AF448837

THE HISTORY OF WORLD MUSIC

Marianna Lima
The History of World Music

All rights reserved
Copyright © 2023 by Marianna Lima

No part of this publication may be reproduced, distributed, or transmitted in any form or by any means, including photocopying, recording, or other electronic or mechanical methods, without the prior written permission of the publisher, except in the case of brief quotations embodied in critical reviews and certain other noncommercial uses permitted by copyright law.

Published by BooxAi
ISBN: 978-965-578-337-7

THE HISTORY OF WORLD MUSIC

MARIANNA LIMA

BOOK'S PURPOSE

The purpose of the book "The History of World Music" is to develop the knowledge of music history among all people in different corners of the world who love music and want to know where their favorite musical styles came from and how they have developed over time.

INTRODUCTION

Hello dear friends. I am happy to meet you again within the framework of my new book. This is my fifth book and the second published in New York City. As you know, I'm a singer first of all, and a traveler; I'm also a writer of my songs; currently, I'm doing my best to establish myself as a singer in the US, and in the future, I'm planning to go back to my traveling life again, from Australia to Africa, this time not alone, but with the companion of my life...

Anyway... now I would like to return to our beautiful book. This time I have taken an interesting and beautiful topic, which is the history of some branches and styles of music, which I am sure will be of interest primarily to music lovers, but why not, also to people who just want to increase their knowledge about the history of music. I have decided to take the main directions of music in order to also explain to you, dear friends, where and how music began to take its place of honor on our planet...

Music is actually a divine force that has its distinct purpose in each of our lives. I can't imagine anyone living more than a few days without music.

It is spiritual food, a doctor who does not need to go to university and get a degree to have the right to heal people. Many times it is even a better doctor and psychologist than a real doctor and psychologist, and many times a better friend or mentor than anyone else....

My previous book "Doctor Music" is about music therapy; I recommend you get it and read it. It has many answers to your questions...

And now, I will begin to tell you about the development of musical origins...

THE BACKGROUND OF THE MUSIC

It is estimated that modern humans appeared for the first time in Africa 160,000 years ago. About 50,000 years ago, people began to settle on all the continents of the earth. All nations of the world, even the most isolated tribes, possess some form of music. Scientists have found that music was even present on planet Earth with people living in Africa before they settled on the planet.

Music is believed to have existed here for 50,000 years and gradually became an integral part of people's lives...

Prehistoric or primitive music is called the oral musical tradition.

Modern American and Australian aboriginal music is also called prehistoric, which is usually applied to European music. The terms folk or traditional music are often used for pre-human music from some European continents. By the way, the flute is the oldest musical instrument. Next to the ancient sculptures, an example of a flute appeared, dating back to BC. 35-40 thousand years.

OLD WORLD MUSIC

The prehistoric era of ancient Greek music ended with the transition to a written musical tradition. The next era is called "Old World Music". The oldest song recorded on a cuneiform tablet was found during the excavations at Niptur in 2000 BC.

Double trumpets and bagpipes were used by the ancient Greeks.

Indian classical music, Marda, can be found in the scriptures of the Veda Music began to spread in Iran in BC 2500-644. History shows that they had a very rich musical culture. Music also played an important role in Egypt. This is evidenced by the ancient Egyptian temples and the murals of the tombs belonging to musicians. The earliest musical instruments of the Egyptians were the harp and the flute. And here, during the new kingdom, the Egyptians played bells, tambourines, drums, and lyres, which were imported from Asia. It is believed that the music of Ancient Greece reached its highest peak in the culture of the Ancient World. It was in ancient Greece that a regular relationship between height and number was first noted, the discovery of which is attributed to Pythagoras.

Music, as an educational subject, and an integral part of social life, was of great importance to the Greeks and, in the future, to some European civilizations.

EARLY MUSIC

Early music is a term used to describe music in the European classical tradition from the fall of the Roman Empire in 476 to the end of the Baroque era in the mid-18th century. Music during this vast period was extremely diverse and included a fusion of many cultures and a wide geographical spread. Many of the cultural groups from which medieval Europe developed already had musical traditions, but about which we know little.

In the Middle Ages, the unifying beginning of these cultures was the Roman Catholic Church. His music emerged as the center of musical development during the first few thousand years of this period. Fortunately for us, the early music of the world has been preserved in a large number of musical sources.

MEDIEVAL MUSIC

According to the facts that have reached us, medieval music was very rich until the 800s AD. However, the history still survives mainly in Roman Catholic liturgical music, which includes the Gregorian chant named after Pope Gregory the First. Historians say that most of the Gregorian chants belonged to unknown authors.

In the 9th century, several important events in the development of medieval music took place. First, the Catholic Church began to make efforts to unify the various directions of Gregorian chant. The second major event was the emergence of early polyphonic music. Octave doubling began to be used, replacing church melody accompaniment through the 2nd voice, forming major intervals from unison to quanta/double-voiced/. Organum or diaphony, the third and most important event, was an attempt to recreate the musical innovation that succeeded after the end of the hundred years of old research by composers in this field.

For the first time, lines were used to write notes. They started using seven or fifteen letters of the Latin alphabet.

The founder of modern musical notation is Guido Aretinsky.

After 1100, several schools of music began to emerge.

1. The school of the monastery of Saint-Martial.

2. The School of Notre Dame, which gave the world high standards of diversity at the time and became the first school of European choral polyphony.

3. The School of Santiago de Compostela was a center for pilgrims and a workplace for composers of many musical traditions in the late Middle Ages.

4. The English School as represented in the Old Hull Manuscripts.

Along with these schools of church music, there were also secular trends in the development of medieval music, which were reflected in many works of composers. The musical forms and aesthetic ideas of the secular musicians of the time initiated the development of early Renaissance music. Unfortunately, however, many pieces of music were destroyed during the Albigensian Crusade at the beginning of the 13th century.

MAIN MUSICAL STYLES

There are four main musical streams: folk music, spiritual music, academic music, and pop music. Each of them also has separate directions.

Folk Music

Folk music is a part of the art, culture, and folklore of every nation. It is passed down from generation to generation.

Traditional classical folk music, mainly created by the rural population, has been relatively independent for a long time; it is opposed to young music. Since folk music is known in all socio-historical formations, written and oral, it should be considered a branch of musical art. It is one of the major branches that contrasts pop and academic music.

Spiritual Music

Spiritual music is associated with religious texts intended for church service or simply for performance in everyday life. Spiritual music generally includes the music of the Christian church. It has many themes, such as African-American spiritual music, gospel, Gregorian chant, mass, Catholic music, apostolic or Greek spiritual music, Indian spiritual music, etc. I will cover some of these types in more detail soon.

Academic Music

It is very interesting that academic music arose from the amalgamation of European and Christian spiritual music. The Christian Church, together with its philosophy and ethics, removes from itself almost all the emotion of the old songs and dances.

Unlike folk music, church singing is self-centered.

Western Christian songs tend toward a higher timbre, while Russian church songs feature a lower timbre. Christian songs are very different from Muslim songs and music. Muslim songs have rougher sounds. Starting from the 17th century, large concert halls began to be built in Europe for the performance of musical arts.

If the Christian church music tried to extract human emotions from the songs, then over time, the academic music did.

Academic music has many genres:

Medieval - Gregorian chant, ars antiqua, early polyphony, School of Notre Dame, etc.

Modernism- impressionism expressionism futurism intuitive music minimalist music etc.

Orchestral music - march, wedding march, spiritual march, symphonic music, spiritual, etc.

Classicism - early and late classicism.

Romanticism - Early Romanticism, Neo-Gothic, and Late Romanticism.

Academic musical genres can be discussed and discussed at great length. They are diverse...

Pop Music

For the first time, the expression "Pop song" was used in 1926, but the roots of pop music are deeper. Pop music has its roots in folk musicians, street romances, and ballads.

Modern pop music developed at the same time as other genres, such as rock music. In the 1950s and 60s, the more popular form was traditional pop, also called pop. Pop from different countries also had a certain mix with that country's music. For example, in the USA, Frank Sinatra combined it with jazz; in France, it was mixed with chanson. And here in the United States, talented African-American performers later had a great influence and created soul music, which I will also talk about.

Obviously, television had a great influence on the development of pop music.

Now I would like to specifically address the most interesting musical directions for me, which I also perform myself...

Gospel Music

Gospel music is a traditional genre of Christian music. The creation, production, and meaning of gospel music are very different from other genres. It includes religious or ritual goals, emotions, and feelings.

Mostly gospel music has very beautiful vocal parts, which I like a lot and perform myself. I even have a song written for me, "Mercy on Me," which you can find online.

In gospel music, songs often have a question-and-answer format. It contains the traditions of African music. When people perform gospel songs, they mostly rely on hand claps and foot stomps. Most of the songs are performed acapella. The first so-called "Gospel Song" was performed in 1874.

Such talented authors as George F. Root, Phillip Bliss, Charles H Gabriel, William Moward, Fanny Crosby, and others have composed in the gospel genre.

Later, gospel music publishing houses also emerged.

The advent of the radio in 1920 had a great impact on the development of music.

After World War II, gospel music moved to mainstream audiences, and concerts took on a more elaborate form. The amalgamation of African-Americans and the Southern Gospel was a major influence on many other musical styles that we have today, such as soul music.

Gospel music in the 18th century

Perhaps the most famous gospel songs were composed in the 1760s and 1770s. Among the early founders were John Newton, author of Amazing Grace, as well as Augustus Toplady, author of Rock of Ages. They were members of the Church of England.

Gospel music in the 19th century

In 1874 Philip Bliss released a collection of songs entitled "Gospel Songs." It included a new style of church music, songs that were more catchy and easier to sing than traditional church hymns. Renowned singers and leaders, including D. Sankey, were involved in the revival movement. By the way, the original works of these talented songwriters can now be found in many libraries.

The popularity of Renaissance singers in rural churches led to the creation of the Gospel Music Publishing Foundation in the 19th and 20th centuries. Thanks to this organization, the works of many songwriters became famous.

This was certainly the most magical period for the Gospel.

Creation of Black Gospel (1920-70)

The Pentecostal movement created fertile conditions for this music over the years. From the 1930s, Black Gospel flourished.

In 1964, the Evangelia Association was created, which in turn started The Dove Awards in 1969. Parallel to this, the Gospel "speech hall" was opened.

In the late 20th Century, musicians such as Elvis Presley, Jerry Leon, and the Blackwood brothers also had gospel-style recordings.

Contemporary Black Gospel and Gospel Rap (1970s - present)

Modern black gospel emerged in the 1970s and continues to this day. The famous song "Oh Happy Day" by Edwin Hawkins Singers has come down to us from this period.

From this time till now, we have very good gospel songs by Yolanda Adams, Kirk Franklin, who is very popular and loved among people. Also, it is very interesting to see the growth of gospel rap and hip hop, which is still growing today.

Most people are aware of many hip-hop stars today, but few know that the roots of hip-hop also come primarily from gospel music.

I recommend getting acquainted with this music because Gospel music contains a lot of strength, optimism, and hope...

Jazz Music

Well, we have come to perhaps the most interesting branch of music for me - Jazz. Jazz music contains American rhythms, European harmonies, as well as African American and Latin American folklore.

The first signs of jazz appeared in the early 19th century in New Orleans. By the way, traveling there was a great pleasure for me. I went to New Orleans for my book "The American Dream," and I really liked Bourbon Street. New Orleans is located in Louisiana on the banks of the River.

The city administration allowed the prisoners to gather outside the square, which later became known as DES Negres and was later renamed Place Kongo;

At this time, the power belonged to the Americans, as the city expanded beyond the borders of the French Quarter, which by then was already called Congo Square.

New Orleans differed from other colonies in its cultural development. More open views of life prevailed here. People appreciated good food, wine, music, and dancing.

Festivals were often organized here. The governor even said that people were already out of control with the dance. The northern part of America was occupied mainly by Protestants in the 18th and 19th centuries. They immigrated from England, Germany, and Holland. Among them were many religious missionaries who wanted to destroy the Christians and introduce these people into their culture. Catholics from France, Spain moved to the southern and central parts.

In New Orleans, they followed the Black Code, which was more lenient than the laws of the British colonies. However, none of them allowed slaves to gather. Their freedom was limited. They could meet on Sundays until 1817. That place was basically Congo Square.

Congo Square was actually the most important culturally rich layer. True jazz, according to many scholars of French, Spanish and American cultures, originated from accumulating.

Slaves made up 30 percent of New Orleans' population in 1721 and nearly 50 percent by the end of the century. Africans used to gather in this square; field workers, domestic servants, children, etc., from different strata of the city.

A group of musicians played cylindrical drums made of animal skins about 30 cm in diameter, sitting on them and pressing their knees together.

Some played homemade stringed instruments shaped like gourds, others struck short sticks and created complex improvisational rhythms.

Here, 500-600 slaves, sometimes several thousand, would gather here in a circle only thirty meters in diameter and move in a circle, stamping their feet and singing songs.

Musicians and dancers were in the center, and people around.

There was a lot of ritual in these dances, and elements of the African parish dance often depended on the emotions of the people.

The beginning of Jazz in 1890-1917

After the closing of Storyville, jazz began to transform from a regional folk genre into a national musical trend, spreading throughout the northern and southern parts of the United States. It also spread to St. Louis, Kansas City, and Memphis.

Ragtime was created in Memphis in the 19th century and spread throughout North America from 1890-1903. Many jazz performers began their careers in minstrel shows.

Jazzmen also began to decline and sing jazz on ships. In the 1920s, Chicago became the main center of jazz development.

A distinct jazz style was formed here, which was called Chicago jazz.

The main directions of Jazz

New Orleans Jazz

This style, as the name suggests, comes from New Orleans, 1900-1917. Its development was facilitated by New Orleans musicians who played in Chicago. This is considered to be the Jazz Age, which in some respects has also been preserved here and has undergone changes.

Swing

Swing means swinging. It is a characteristic type of pulsation based on constant deviations of the rhythm.

This creates an unstable state of impression of our internal energy. Orchestral jazz emerged in the 1920s and 30s, however, as a result of a synthesis of European styles.

Symphonic Jazz

Symphonic jazz emerged in the 1920s in the United States as a result of a fusion of European, Latin American, and African cultures. In the first half of the 20th century, the migration of millions of people from different countries of the world to America led to the interaction of different cultures and the creation of new musical trends. Representatives of classical music brought their culture from Europe to the US, many musicians who were trained in European universities brought their culture here, and many of them found work in Hollywood. They also played in restaurants and dance floors, and all this contributed to the creation and development of this new style. The most famous white jazzman is George Gershwin. He was a native of New York to a Jewish family who had emigrated from the Russian Empire. If you are interested, definitely read about Gershwin, and I also recommend listening to his music.

Bebop

This type of jazz developed in the early 20th century in the mid-40s in New York and thus opened the modern jazz era. It is characterized by a fast tempo and complex improvisations based on changes in harmony rather than melody.

The breakneck pace of the performance was set by Charlie Parker and Gillespie.

In contrast to swinging, which is mainly the music of commercial big dance bands, Bebop is an experimental creative direction of jazz, mainly associated with the practice of small ensembles, and in this regard, it was a smooth transition from popular dance music to a more practical, intellectual, but more obscure for many people. It contains complex improvisations.

As I mentioned, Charlie Parker, trumpeter Dizzy Gillespie, pianists Bud Powell and Thelonious Monk, and drummer Max Rose are among the founders of Bebop.

Big Band

This form of jazz emerged in the 1920s and lasted until the late 1940s. Musicians who played in huge big bands, mostly in their teens, mostly played specific parts and also learned new parts during rehearsals. Huge brass and woodwind ensembles combined to create rich jazz harmonies, creating a sensationally loud sound that later became known as the big band sound. The big band reached its prime. Although many bands declined after World War II, many albums were recorded in this style.

This style was gradually replaced by new trends.It was given improvisational freedom. Today, the big band is the standard of jazz education.

Mainstream Jazz

Big-band jazz was very trendy during this period of time. But people also liked to hear swing, especially in the smaller clubs in New York. This style was a combination of traditional swing and endless imaginative improvisations. Many jazz stars performed compositions in this style at jam sessions.

Today, mainstream jazz is any approach to jazz that is far from classical jazz.

It contains a freedom that allows many jazzmen to come up with new renditions.

North American Jazz - Stride

Although the history of jazz began in the 20th century, jazz music experienced its true rise in the 1920s.

Louis Armstrong, the famous trumpeter, and singer, left New Orleans to create new music in Chicago. Many talented musicians from New Orleans also migrated to New York. Jazz flourished in Chicago thanks to musicians such as Jimmy McPartland, Eddie Condon, Art Hodes, Barrett Deems, and Benny Goodman. Armstrong and Goodman eventually moved to New York and developed the music there.

Chicago became the number 1 center for jazz recordings, and New York opened the most famous clubs, Playhouse, Cotton Club, Savog, Village verge word, also Carnegie Hall.

Kansas City Style

During the Great Depression, the Kansas City style brought new sounds in the 1920s and 30s. This style includes blues notes. It is performed by both large groups and small ensembles. It includes many energetic soloists. This style was mostly performed in pubs where illegal liquor was sold. It was here that Count Basie's style emerged in Walter Paley's orchestra, then also in Benny Mouten's orchestra.

These two orchestras typified the typical Kansas City style.

It had a unique approach to the blues, which was later called "Urban Blues." I will cover the blues style in more detail later. I perform blues music myself, and I really like this unique style.

Jimmy Rushing is a famous singer performing in the Kansas City style, Charlie Parker, a famous alto-saxophonist born in Kansas City, also played a major role in the creation of some jazz styles, as I mentioned. He made extensive use of typical blues techniques. I definitely recommend listening to his music...

West Coast Jazz

West Coast Jazz was born in the 1950s by cool jazz artists. They are mostly recorded in Los Angeles studios. Here came a very talented jazzman, Miles Davis, who created a new style called West Coast Jazz. Miles Davis is very popular to this day and is a mentor to many musicians.

The most famous of the recording studios was Lighthouse, The Huige, where the best studios of the time recorded.

Cool Jazz

Bebop's high intensity and pressure began to wane with the development of cool jazz. Beginning in the 1940s and 1950s, musicians began to develop a more fluid approach to improvisation.

Trumpeter Miles Davis was one of the first performers of cool jazz.

Zet Baker, pianist George Shearing, and others were also not far behind them.

It has a certain dissonance, a muted character. Of course, this type also has its followers to this day. Personally, I also really like Miles Davis' approach to cool jazz.

Progress Jazz

On the basis of bebop jazz, a new type of jazz was born, which was Progress Jazz. The main difference of this genre is the departure from the frozen clichés of beats, the contradictory type of which can be seen in symphonic jazz.

Here, in symphonic jazz, the effort is more to improve the expressions of the rhythms, practically introducing the composition into tone and harmony.

This is one of the latest achievements of the European symphony. The greatest contribution to the development of this style, Progress Jazz, was made by pianist and conductor Stan

Kenton, who was composing in the 1940s. His compositions were in some ways close to those of Rachmaninoff.

They had an air of romanticism and were close to the symphony. He later released the album "Artisty," which was not so rich in jazz colors. There were many musicians working in this genre which are still popular today.

Hard Jazz

Well, we all know what "hard" means. This type originated from the 1950 bop. It differs in expressive, harsher sounds, closer to blues.

This type of jazz found more popularity in Detroit, Philadelphia, and New York. It was a little far from the standard forms of jazz. Here, fiery vocal performances and improvisational mastery with the performance of brass and percussion instruments pushed the piano further into the background; the bass moved into a more playful mood. Blues lovers will also like this jazz type.

Modal Jazz

Beginning in the 1950s, Miles Davis, pianist Bill Avon, and tenor saxophonist John Coltbein pioneered experiments with diatonic modes, also typical of Spanish and Indian music.

This resulted in the modal jazz genre. Here, the rhythm can be changed, which gives the performers a lot of room for improvisation.

Many times the performers used exotic elements in this genre from Indian, Arabic, and African music.

This music has a meandering nature, and the rhythm and tonal play is typical of this type of jazz and does not allow the listeners to get bored...

Soul Jazz

This music is one of my favorite styles. It mainly contains afro american music and blues modulations. Blues traditions and African-American folklore are the mainstays of soul music. It was very close to hard jazz in style, characterized by modal sounds based on small mini-compositions that emerged in the 1950s and continued to be performed until the 1970s. The fusion of blues and gospel misfits has a true African-American feel to it. Many jazz songwriters got their start in soul music. Among them were Jimmy McGreeve, Charles Earland, Richard Holmes, Les McGreeve, Donald Patterson, and others. In the 1960s, many bands played in clubs as a trio; the tenor saxophone was also very important in ensembles, playing the role of gospel preaching voice. Soul was different from west-coast jazz. It has more passion and melody. And that the west coast contained more coldness.

This style was more accessible to people and has become very popular to this day. Although today's soul jazz is slightly different from true soul as it is more pop-oriented, the basics are the same. Personally, this style is very close to my soul; I even have songs specially written for me in the soul style, with which I won many international competitions and festivals. If we discuss the soul artists of today, Aretha Franklin stands in first place for me. Unfortunately, she passed away years ago, but her songs remain in our hearts forever...

Neo-soul

Neo-soul formed in the late 1990s. It is close to classic soul; it includes elements of alternative hip-hop, jazz, and even classical music. Neo-soul remains perhaps the relatively unpopular, relatively modern rhythm and blues. Representatives of its more commercial type are Usher, Justin Timberlake, and Beyonce, who are still very popular and recognized. I myself have songs written in this style. Because it allows you to express certain vocal possibilities, lyrics, and emotion, and at the same time, has more modern instrumentation, which allows you to gather a large audience...

Well, dear friends, maybe that's all about the soul. And I move on to the next interesting musical style.

Funk Jazz

Funk jazz is a branch of soul jazz that contains elements of blues.

Funk jazz has an exceptional rhythmic focus.

It is sometimes also referred to as a groove, where there is a light instrumental influence on the maintenance of the rhythmic pattern, sometimes with lyrical cues.

Jazz-funk-style compositions are full of happy emotions. It is sometimes dance and has fast or slow forms. Solo improvisations strictly obey the beat and the collective voice.

Among the most famous representatives of this style are Richard Holmes, Shirshi Squat, tenor saxophonist Jean Emmons, alto saxophonist, and flutist Leo Wright. It has a very good effect on mood. If you were not familiar with funk-jazz before today, be sure to get acquainted.

Free Jazz

Perhaps the most controversial movement in jazz history emerged with the advent of Free Jazz. Although these types of elements existed in the musical structure of jazz long before the term was coined, the most original were some of the musicians who developed a unique style of free jazz: Coleman Hodwins, Lenny Tristano, Ornette Coleman, and others...

The difference with Free jazz is that it was an innovation in jazz with imagination and great musicality, which was far from chordal progression, and all this made it possible to move in any direction. In that type, the pacing meter is no longer significantly different, and the tonality can be changed.

Creative Jazz

The emergence of Creative Jazz was marked by a distinct blend of experimentalism and avant-gardeism. The beginning of this process also coincided with the creation of Free Jazz. Elements of avant-garde jazz, understood as certain changes in music and innovations, have always been experimental.

And so, from the 1950s to the 70s, this type of jazz evolved by introducing a new image of tonality and rhythm structure. It's actually very close to free jazz. Here the compositional part is connected to the improvisation, and it is difficult to understand where the first part ends and the second part begins. It has a quadratic sound and a very interesting sound. Representatives of this type are pianist Lenny Dristano, saxophonist Jimmy Joffrey, and conductor Gunter Schuller.

Fusion Jazz

Fusion was formed in the 1960s in conjunction with pop and rock. By the way, I will talk about rock music a little later. It is based on: soul, funk, blues. It originally had the name jazz-rock. It had such elements as electronics and rock rhythms. During the performance of the music, emphasis is placed on improvisations that are also melodic.

This style of music sounds very melodic even today. Representatives include Ronald Shannon Jackson, James Elmer, Ornette Coleman, and others…

Post Bop Jazz

The Post Bop genre of jazz arose mainly from musicians who drew on Bebop. It was created in the 1960s as a result of jazz experiments. It is based on the energy ensemble structure of wind instrument combinations and Latin elements.

It's very different from funk, soul… in its structure and energy. It also goes well with pop music. There are masters like Moblin, Art Blakey himself, and Lee Morgan. They were very influential in the development of post-bop. Here, with simpler melodies and a soulful rhythm, the listener can also hear gospel and blues sounds. In the 1960s, this style was used as a composition to create a variety of new structures.

Acid Jazz

This type of jazz is already very interesting by its name. This term is used a lot in very broad musical circles.

Acid jazz emerged from the funk style in 1987 to be used in British pubs. It also contains terms from classical jazz and Latin jazz occasionally.

In fact, this style is a variation of the jazz revival, which is more inspired by the records of the 60s. Over time, after the formative phase of this style, improvisation disappeared, which caused conflicts among jazzmen who wanted to understand whether acid jazz was a real type of jazz.

An early representative of acid jazz is Jumiroquai, the James Taylor quartet, and others. Acid jazz sounds very interesting even today, be sure to listen...

Smooth Jazz

Smooth Jazz evolved from fusion. It contains energetic solos, dynamic crescendos, as well as a combination of some sounds from the main older types of jazz.

Improvisations don't happen that often here.

It is separated from more lively jazz performances. Smooth jazz uses drums, guitar, bass guitar, alto, or soprano saxophone.

Smooth jazz is definitely a more upbeat form after the swing era.

This type of jazz is very popular today. Kenny J, Dave Cole, Larry Carlbone, and others have had great success in it.

I can talk endlessly about jazz music. In fact, this is one of my favorite types... The history of jazz shows that this is a form that should have existed on our planet, and without this musical form, the world's musical stock would be incomplete...

This also applies to other styles of music, such as classical music, rock, why not pop...

Well, let's move on and talk about other types of music.

But before that, I would like to share with you some interesting facts about jazz...

1. April 30 is International Jazz Day. It was defined by UNESCO in 2011.

Art Blakey said, "Jazz clears away the dust from the worries of everyday life, from the worries of everyday life," and it's hard to disagree with him.

2. The name Jazz does not have any deep roots. It has several different opinions.

There is a hypothesis that jazz means to make love, "jazzbo," jazz baby, jazzing, and all these words are related to love. It also defines "affordable cinema" production. According to some legends, this term was first used by Clarence Williams and in his works. Then over time, it started to be used in colloquial language.

3. Although jazz was originally considered black music, it is actually rooted in many musical styles, from European chamber music to Afrobeat. I already talked about this a while ago. It's just that jazz would not exist without classical music, for which we should be grateful to our talented European composers and musicians.

4. One of the most used jazz instruments is the saxophone. However, this Belgian instrument was originally created for the chamber orchestra. And the Brown Brothers brought it to the USA for the first time.

5. Jazz lovers today are people leading more elite lives, more intellectual, and higher in quality of life. In their time, it was the exact opposite. It used to be done mainly for the lower class, where it was insanely insecure. It's very interesting how things have changed over time...

6. Jazz actually has over 40 subgroups. I have mentioned the most popular ones, but they also have ramifications.

7. A very interesting experience for me is that the brains of jazz musicians are more active. Two professors from John Hawkins University came to this conclusion.

They found out that when performing jazz, the human brain emits impulses in the prefrontal and occipital orbital regions, which are responsible for harmony and self-control. This part, in turn, sends signals to the part of the prefrontal cortex that is responsible for free expression.

So singing or playing jazz is also very healthy. I have tested myself and completely agree with this idea.

8. Argentinian tango Charleston came to America thanks to jazz. The redevelopment and development of public dance spaces are directly related to the birth of jazz because it was originally dance music.

9. In fact, before the advent of jazz, women had different social ranks. It was during the heyday of jazz that women started going to bars, drinking, smoking, and dressing more openly.

By the way, at this time, women got the right to vote in elections, which is also very symbolic...

I think many of you are familiar with F. Scott Fitzgerald's The Great Gatsby. If not, I definitely recommend reading it or maybe watching the movie. In fact, F. Scott Fitzgerald was accompanied by the Jazz Age, the so-called Jazz Age, and he was the first to use the Jazz Era.

Well, friends, I think I managed to get you interested enough to start getting familiar with some jazz works... it will definitely be useful for you, believe me...

And I move on to the next musical style.

Rock Music

When saying rock, unique emotions arise in every person, making them more lively and energetic.

An integral part of rock music is the bass guitar and drums, which provide a clear energy to this music. Rock music emerged in the 1950s. Today it has a history of more than 70 years, which is full of events and facts.

The USA became the birthplace of Rock. People immigrated here from different parts of the world: Britain, Africa, and Europe. Each of them brought their culture with them and developed it in the United States.

Rock is basically a complaint.

Almost all political decisions, wars, and historical and religious disagreements took place in this music. As new musical trends emerged from the mix of African-American alto rhythms, the more conservative population did not take these styles as seriously. They called this "slave music."

But the newly created rock and roll found a large audience. Perhaps because of the protests against this conservatism, young people actively preferred new styles. It was this category of Americans who brought blacks to the big stage and to the concert music scene. European musicians were also interested in this new style.

They started experimenting with this style. And unlike the more closed pop music of the era, rock music preached more freedom, which shocked humanity in that conservative era. In the 60s, the Rolling Stones appeared, expanded the boundaries of rock, and began recording albums in addition to singles. They preached freedom, which caused much controversy, but nevertheless made them famous.

As rock music became a dynamic form of pop music, new bands took advantage of the musicians that came before them.

For example, Led Zepplin gave rock a darker and heavier character, becoming the most popular band of the 70s, and also laid the foundation for its own style, which was hard rock and heavy metal.

By the 1980s, the classic rock form had lost its commercial potential and began to sound older.

Some bands inspired by punk, such as Depeche Mode, started making music in the post-punk style, which gave rise to a new wave. At this time, American bands such as REM began to combine post-punk with rock. This style was called college rock.

In 1991, Nirvana released the alternative album "Nevermind," which was very successful.

But after the suicide of Nirvana frontman Kurt Cobain, alternative music began to lose its luster. New groups began to emerge, such as Limp Bizkit, who brought together hard rock, pop, gibrit, and rap-rock.

Staind, Puddle of Mudd, and Limp Bizkit were also popular. They performed more melodic hard rock. As rock music matured in the 21st century, bands had an air similar to the air of the 60s. The famous group Linkin Park combined hip-hop with metal. The band Door Down followed the traditions of hard rock but, at the same time, had a new breath.

I personally like to listen to and perform melodic rock performances.

I would also like to mention some interesting facts about rock.

1. The Doors were the first band in the world to display their new album on a billboard.

2. Scientists have discovered that rock has a very good effect on brain function and intelligence. Not even any style of music affects our brains like that.

3. In Sweden, people are considered to have an addictive, unhealthy approach to rock. They call these people disabled.

4. Few people know that Metallica's music was used to torture captured Iraqis. Moreover, the leader of the group openly supported such practices.

5. Human hearing can simultaneously perceive 85 decibels of sound without causing any health damage. But at rock concerts, the volume sometimes exceeds 120.

6. I advise you to stay away from dynamics during rock concerts to avoid hearing damage.

7. The parts played in Radiohead's "Creep" were just received by John Greenwood during a rehearsal, and he didn't intend to use

it, but the effect was so good that fans liked it, and it became a favorite sound.

8. Steve Vai has a very unusual hobby. He is a beekeeper, and the money he earns from the honey goes directly to a fund fighting cancer called "Make a Noise."

9. The title of Led Zeppelin's song "Black Dog" comes from the story of a black labrador dog entering the studio during the recording of the song.

10. Queen's frontman Brian May played a self-made guitar that he called the Red Special throughout his career. He built this guitar with his father over the course of two years.

So... this is it about rock music. And I am moving on to the history of the next style.

Country Music

Country music genre is very popular in the USA. This is the so-called American country music that originated among white people. It is mainly composed of song and dance tunes brought by settlers from Europe, mainly in North America.

The term country music was first used in the 1940s. But in the beginning, this style was called hillbilly music. It was mainly based on Anglo-Celtic folk music.

This music was preserved intact for a long time.

Among amateur musicians in the Highlands of Tennessee, Kentucky, and North Carolina, country music songs and ballads are similar in nature to themes typical of rural folklore.

These songs use a lot of guitars. By the way, Mandolin was often used before that, as well as the violin, which by the way, was the main instrument of American farmers for centuries.

The influence of the culture of Afro-American music was most clearly manifested in the rhythm and in the random improvisation method of performance, the use of the harmonica. Thanks to widespread radio, country music became very popular in the United States. Country music tends to have a multi-guitar chord rhythm in 2/4 or 4/4. The vocal part is usually followed by a choral refrain. The United States is considered to have no specific folk music. But it is Kentucky-based country music that is the main birthplace of this music.

Wayne Erbsen once said:

"It is generally believed that America has no folk music, nothing distinctively native out of which a national school of advanced composition may arise. But there is hidden among the mountains of Kentucky... a people of whose inner nature and musical expression almost nothing has been said."

He notes that the highlanders of the Southeast welcomed improvements that made their lives easier, but they did not seek to improve their culture. The reason for this was the persistence of immigrants from Scotland, Ireland, and Germany who settled in the mountains. Musical and dance traditions were really rooted in them; when the violinists chose a tune for the dances, they always chose from the tunes they were familiar with.

When drummers in the United States began playing old folk songs on the radio in the 1920s and recording them on gramophone records, the commercial approach was limited to the folk and country genres. Country records began in the 1920s. One of the first recorded songs was Henry C Gilliland and A C Robertson Arkansas Traveler (1922).

After the establishment of radio, first amateur and then professional country music festivals began to be organized.

Phonographic discs began to be recorded in stadiums, marking the beginning of the commercialization of the genre.

Country performers became popular and loved by the public.

What is the secret of the phenomenalism of this genre? In fact, the country genre can be recognized from the very first chords. The songs are filled with mostly deep meaning. They tell life stories. Acoustic accompaniment is usually accompanied by a guitar, fiddle, banjo or harmonica. Country music vocalists are mostly representatives of academic styles.

The country also has species.

1. Alt-Country- This is a more modern type of country. It's more aggressive, modern than a traditional country. It has certain gothic undertones.

2. Western swing- Early country had blues, jazz, and swing tunes. It had a richer and denser sound and used a Hawaiian guitar here.

3. Bluegrass, an interesting subgenre, has African motifs and is also a mixture of Scottish, Irish, and English musical traditions.

The special romanticism characteristic of the country contains a national philosophy. It continues to evolve. It sounds very warm and creates an interesting, intimate atmosphere. I like this style, I don't have any songs written in this style yet, but maybe I will in the future.

Chamber Music

It is one of my favorite genres in chamber music. Chamber music has many meanings.

Chamber- being in art means limiting yourself in a certain way because this style has many rules.

Chamber music is performed in the presence of a certain number of musicians- two to twelve who play different parts at the same time without games and unison.

The history of Chamber Music

The history of chamber music began in the 15th century. It was during this period that a demand arose among the wealthier class to create noble music. That is, not the music that was already performed in churches and had a religious connotation, but some style that would sound richer and more professionally processed. Musicians were offered to play in small rooms, living rooms. This is why it is called a camera. Translated from Latin, it means camera- room.

Of course, this music sounds more bare than orchestral because most of the time it has three to four instruments. However, this was what distinguished this style from the church style, which had an exclusive approach. No recording capabilities existed at this time. And this music could only be heard live, that's why people perceived it in a completely different way than chamber music; the seats of the audience are usually very close together, and it creates a more intimate situation. Also, the audience is generally seated very close to the musicians.

In 1635 Italian composer Giacomo Arrigoni released his collection "Concerti la camera."

Later, vocals were also used in the chamber genre.

Later in the 18th century, greater distinctions emerged between chamber and church music. Chamber music became an instrumental genre.

A trio sonata with two violins and a bass instrument appeared.

A commercial orchestra must be distinguished from a small orchestra. In the chamber style, also in the 18th century, a combination of 25 musicians was used; in a chamber orchestra, there is a rule - one musician per part. This is a principle for the camera. And in the orchestra, they can perform in small numbers, but the form does not change.

I will also touch on the history of the orchestra.

One of the most famous composers was Handel, who composed for balls, royal parties. His music sounds very transparent and beautiful.

Also, I can't help but mention my favorite, Mozart, who left a very important mark on world music. His music also includes works for commercial orchestras. Compositions by Franz Schubert, Robert Schumann, Frederic Chopin, and Ferenc Liszt also left a big trace on the history of commercial music.

These talented composers have created works that are full of emotion as well as professionalism. Claude Debussy is a famous impressionist composer whose unique approach brought new life to chamber music. I like this style a lot; I definitely recommend visiting concerts related to classical music because not only is it very pleasant to listen to classical music, but it is also very healthy, especially for the brain. Well, enough about chamber music, and I'll move on.

Reggae Music

Reggae is a very interesting music genre. It originated in Jamaica. It gained great popularity in the 1960s and 70s.

Reggae can be relaxing or resisting. It follows African cultural traditions, where rhythm, music, and the history of certain actions are related.

Electric guitar, bass guitar, percussion instruments, and sometimes brass instruments are used here. 4/4 measure is mostly present in reggae.

The king of reggae is Bob Marley, who still has a huge army of fans.

By the way, reggae has an interesting history. Mento music was more popular in Jamaica in the 20th century. The performers of this music were mostly refugees who had an energetic approach to Caribbean music, a freer, melodic approach. It was like American blues.

After World War 2, Jamaica was flooded with new musical trends, mainly from the United States.

In 1950, a phenomenon called the Jamaica Soundsystem was created in Jamaica. Most of humanity lived very poor and did not have the opportunity to own a musical instrument. Some people made some dynamics themselves at home and used them on the streets. In the 1950s, some celebrities started opening music studios that had some equipment. Musicians who performed on the streets began to record in these studios. It was from this time that the Jamaican music scene began to develop. The main center was Kensington. In the 1960s, the fusion of SKA with Gospel created a new style that also influenced reggae. Gradually, this music began to spread in the USA and Europe.

During this period, black people were fighting for their rights, which resulted in the creation of "Black Power," which also influenced reggae. The soul of the struggle began to be expressed in the songs and found a great victory among the people.

In the 1970s, reggae became a world-famous style, and its king remains Bob Marley.

Interesting facts about Reggae

1. Reggae features a special rhythm called skanking. Here the rhythm takes over everything. The bass acts as a driving force for the music. Jamaican musicians had a special privilege called patua or creole.

2. It is interesting to know where the term reggae came from. In 1968, Toots and the Maytals recorded "Do the reggae," which is actually a first in the genre. And here is the song "Long Shot, Kick de Bucket" by "The Pioneers" group recorded a year ago. This was actually the first hit written in the reggae style, and after these songs became popular and popular, this style was called reggae. And Bob Marley has become a real legend in Jamaica. At his concerts, people treated him like a god.

3. In fact, reggae is somewhat of a worldview. In Jamaica, people have their own religion, in which there is a hero, Ras Tafari, who, according to history, was supposed to bring freedom and improvement to mankind. Reggae itself is freedom...

4. Reggae is also heavily associated with marijuana. It is very popular in Jamaica and is considered a symbol of wisdom because it grew on the tomb of Prince Solomon.

5. In 1962 Jamaica gained independence from the United Kingdom. This brought a lot of success in the music scene to the musicians.

6. By the way, Bob Marley died on May 11, 1981, at the age of 30. His house museum today is called Tuff gong international and is a recording studio for students. Hundreds of musicians and tourists from all over the world visit here every year.

Symphonic Music

Symphonic music is music composed for a symphony orchestra. In my view, this type of music is the richest in terms of color and variety of instruments. It also often contains emotional approaches and big musical plays. Sometimes this style is also used for smaller ensembles, both for string instruments and symphonies.

Ensembles and orchestras were active from antiquity to the medieval period. Gradually, vocals were added to the instruments. Symphonic music is also called philharmonic. The name comes from the Greek word "phileo" - to love; in fact, in several countries of the world, the philharmonic concept has the task of organizing concerts to promote the development and advancement of musical art.

The philharmonic movement aims to spread the values of musical art through symphonic music.

In Europe, in the 16th century, the first music academies began to be created, mainly in Italy and then in Germany.

This culture came to the USA and other countries later in the 19th century.

The classical symphony was actually formed in this time period mainly by European composers: Haydn, Mozart, Beethoven, and other very talented composers.

Today, many countries have their own philharmonic orchestras, who sometimes collaborate with jazz and pop singers.

I like to attend concerts of symphony orchestras.

I hope to have a concert with a symphony orchestra soon. So far, I have been given the opportunity to perform live concerts only with a jazz band, which is a very pleasant and interesting job.

Quiet Storm

This trend flattened out in the 1980s and ended the rise in the mid-1990s. This style contains soft, smooth vocals, a romantic mood, and no fast tempo. Many singers perform in this style even today. For example, Whitney Houston, Mariah Carey, Toni Braxton. They started their music career in this style.

Quiet Storm has evolved over time and blended hip-hop with Ritmena Blues slow jam R&B.

Folk Music

Folk music is passed down from generation to generation. Different nations around the world pass on their national traditions and culture. The national music of every country is a part of folk. It was mostly not printed on paper but transmitted orally. National songs also originated as spiritual music and evolved into more everyday culture over time.

This tradition was observed mainly in France, Poland, England, and Germany.

National music has gone through 3 stages of development:

1. In ancient times, when the first human groups appeared on earth and established their own countries and governments over time.

2. National music from medieval culture, when folklore took classical form. This happened first in Europe. There, folk was associated with Christian music.

3. Contemporary - new and cutting-edge, in other words, songs from the history of music. When many countries transitioned to a capitalist system, folk music took on a new form here.

Folk music in every country is unique and has its own way of development.

I have never performed songs in folk style myself, but folk-jazz sounds very interesting to me

Indie Music

The word indie comes from the word independent, which means independent music. In fact, no musical style is as difficult to understand as an indie. It got its name in the 50s and 60s when musicians began to show some creativity, originality, and freedom during recordings. It reached the peak of its development in the 70s. In 1980, the first indie music chart was created in England. It is still very popular and popular today.

Today we know Arctic Monkeys, The Killers, Ashanti, Blur, and other artists performing in this style.

Indie continues to mix with other different styles and get more interesting sounds.

Electronic Music

Electronic music is created with electronic sounding, new technologies mainly by computer.

It was created at the end of the 20th century. By the way, the first recording studio in the world was created in 1857 by Frenchman Édouard-Léon Scott. Then, 20 years later, the American Thomas A. Edison improved it and made it possible for us to have a recording studio, which is of course, a world achievement. Already from the 1940s, electronic music was considered a certain style. The Italian pianist Ferruccio Busoni (1866-1924) played a major role in the development of this music. In 1907 they started using new technologies to get a new sound. Began to use noise as a new sound technique. Without talented and intelligent people, this style would never have developed.

Their names are many: Leon Scott de Martinville, Elisha Gray, William Du Bois, Maurice Martinez, Friedrich Trautwein, and others.

Along with the development of European electronic music, a new style - Tape Music - was developed in the USA in the 50s, whose representatives were Earle Brown, Christian Wolff, David Fodor, Morton Feldman, and John Cage. By the way, Cage and Morton teamed up for "The Music for magnetic tape" project.

The Tape Music Studio was opened at Columbia University in New York, which played a major role in the development of this music. The other recording studios were opened in different corners of the world. In 1977, the IRCAM center was opened in Paris. Stanford University in the USA created the Center for computer research in Music and Acoustics.

The term electronic music itself began to be widely used in the 1970s in various directions: house, trance, techno, etc.

Now I'd like to talk a little bit about each of these styles.

House Music

House's main roots come from Disco Music. A lot of DJs started recording their songs which got people's approval. Club culture became widespread in the 80s. Musicians began to make their instrumentation less melodic, with more repetitive passages and deeper bass accompaniment. Along with all of this came the anti-Disco. The disco Demolition night movement and this music started recording by Major Label Studio at Bryground Club. At this time, this music was still associated with a rich orchestral flute and various brass instruments.

One of the first hits in this style was "I Feel Real Love," published in 1977. Today, House music presents new sounds every time because the technologies have developed a lot compared to before and continue to develop. Famous DJs include Dusky, Mr. Frrankie Hruckles, Green Velvet, Carl Cox, Black Coffee, Hardwell, Vintage Culture, Alesso Chu, Tiesto, and others.

Progressive House

This music genre emerged in the 1990s. In 1992, a record was registered in "Mixmay Dom Phillips" magazine. US-based Italian DJ Sasha played in this style. It was a very popular style in England, containing 120-130 bmp bit. In fact, there is a theory that progressive house wants to return house music to a more melodic classical type.

It energetically seems to hypnotize the human brain. Today it is popular and popular all over the world.

Famous musicians in this style include Will Sparks, EDX, Jim Josef, Jody Wisternoff, Matt Large, Dwin, Matt Fax, and others.

Trance Music

Trance music is considered to be a style of electronic music that got its name due to the smooth transition of bass lines and rhythmic melodies. This musical genre is universal. Formed in the 90s, it has a very light soft tempo; it sounds alive due to its breakdown in the songs; the dada music is missing, which gives it a certain interesting sound.

Trance is very popular in Ibiza, where a new style was formed called the Ibiza trance.

Then other styles developed: acid and PSY trance, Progressive trance, and uplifting trance.

Techno-House Music

Techno House music was first played in UK clubs. Since 1994, it has become very popular.

In 1997, the famous producer Steve Lawler released the CD "Dark Drums," which was in the style of Techno House.

Since 2005, it has acquired a new style called Micro House. It is still very popular and popular today in the USA, Germany, England, Netherlands, etc.

Well, that's all about the house and its other subgenres today, and I'll move on.

Rock and Roll

Rock and Roll literally captured the attention of most Americans starting in the 50s. While young people enjoyed this music in clubs, their parents opposed the development of this style.

The term Rock and Roll was first used by American DJ Alan Dridge. He often played African-American music on the radio and said that young people were drawn to this music. In 1952, there was a song called "Will Rock Will Rock," which is where the name came from.

After World War II, racial problems in the United States worsened. African Americans were not allowed to board a bus if a white American was standing on it. In the southern states of the United States, young people of different skin colors rejoiced together in different places. Until now, the same about the gospel. Their music had no place on the radio. This had very strong roots as this phenomenon came from white people who were still inclined towards classical music only. But the youth demanded freer new music. The King of Rock and Roll is Elvis Presley. When he was drafted into the army in the late 50s, the magazines said Rock and Roll were dead.

But over time, this style showed the world that he was alive. Today, this musical style is mainly performed by individual artists, mainly to preserve the old traditions and to differentiate themselves. Today, many also imitate Elvis Presley; he is still an idol for many. Well, that's all about rock and roll.

Ethnic Music

Ethnic music is a combination of traditional, pop, and folk music.

This music genre evolved from modern and European commercial recording standards.

In the 20th century, such American composers as Henry Kruelya, Jonah Keiza, Lou Harrison, and Alana Hovanes were very important in the development of ethnic music.

In this way, ethnic music is called "world music," which is certainly very diverse and rich in the cultures of different nations.

Throat music is the mainstay of ethnic music, as well as many national instruments.

Many ensembles have wanted to present ethnic music in their own way, including Ethnic Ni Bhraonain, Loreena McKennitt, Michael Hrmek, and others.

Ethnic music, in turn, has other directions.

1. Ethno-jazz - Cuban music, mambo, rumba cha-cha-cha belong to this type.

2. World Fusion - This music genre includes electronic dance music.

Here electronic music is combined with guitar music. It sounds very interesting.

3. Ethno-rock - This is the most popular type of ethno-music. It sounds world beat in English. I definitely recommend listening to this type of music. I think many people will like it.

4. Throat Singing- This style is accompanied by vivid throat vocal performances.

It is also important not to confuse ethnicity with folklore. By the way, I would like to mention some names in this style, the creative duduk player Jivan Gasparyan, Zdob si Zdub, Nino Katamadze, Afion Deep forest Balkanika, Stefan Hertrich, Vivalda, Dula Baka Beyond, Ray Lema and others.

I really like ethno-jazz music, which has a very clean, interesting new sound.

I think that ethno is one of those styles that still has a long way to develop, especially mixing with other styles. Its types are diverse.

EPILOGUE

Well, dear friends, here we are, done with the book "The Story of World Music."

Of course, I missed many musical styles and new genres, but I tried to cover the most important and famous genres and their history.

I hope it was interesting.

See you soon...

Marianna Lima

Marianna Lima is a jazz, soul, gospel blues, and pop singer. Marianna Lima has more than 20 international awards from around the world. She has traveled nearly 30 percent of the planet on her concert and competition tours. Marianna's first three books about the sights and historical and cultural structures of Europe, the USA, and Canada also played a big role in that case.

Marianna Lima published her book "Doctor Music" in March 2023 in New York about music therapy and the healing properties of music. This is Marianna's 5th book on the history of world music.

www.ingramcontent.com/pod-product-compliance
Lightning Source LLC
Chambersburg PA
CBHW051454140726
47987CB00006B/2700